Cheerful Charm
QUILTS

Martingale®
Create with Confidence

Cheerful Charm Quilts

© 2013 by Martingale & Company®

Martingale

19021 120th Ave. NE, Ste. 102
Bothell, WA 98011-9511 USA
ShopMartingale.com

Printed in China
18 17 16 15 14 13   8 7 6 5 4 3 2

Library of Congress Cataloging-in-Publication Data is available upon request.
ISBN: 978-1-60468-343-1

Mission Statement

Dedicated to providing quality products
and service to inspire creativity.

Contents

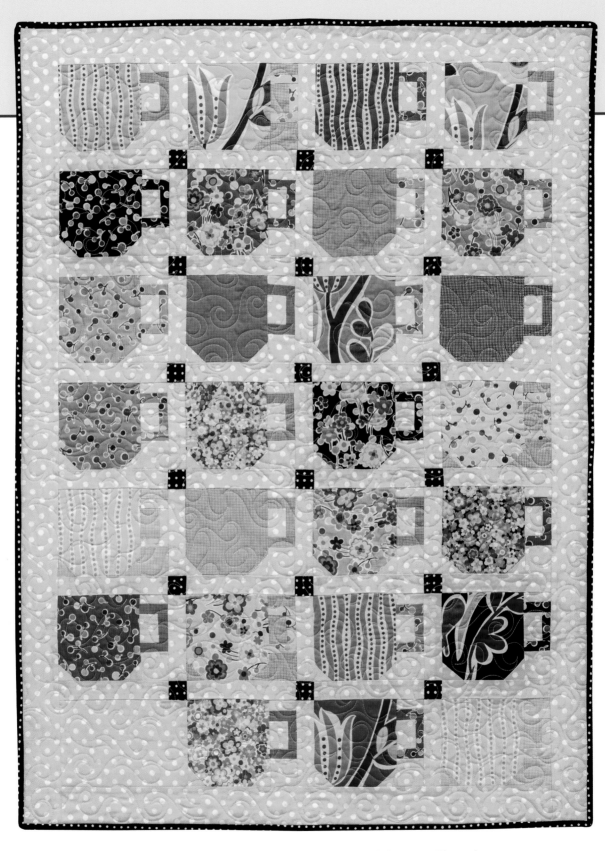

By Mary Etherington and Connie Tesene of Country Threads

Quilt size: 31" x 41½" • Block size: 4½" x 6"

Coffee Shop

With the arrival of Internet cafes and designer roasts, coffee is more popular than ever. Whether your favorite brew comes from an espresso machine or from a can, you'll enjoy making this quilt.

Materials

Yardage is based on 42"-wide fabric. Charm squares are 5" x 5". Instructions are simplified to cut all block backgrounds from the yellow-dotted fabric, but you can cut some from additional contrasting charm squares.

27 assorted charm squares for coffee cups (28 if you don't want a blank square)

10 charm squares for handles (use duplicates and fabrics similar to coffee-cup squares)

1¼ yards of yellow-dotted fabric for sashing, blank square, background, and outer border

⅜ yard of black-dotted fabric for cornerstones and binding

1½ yards of fabric for backing

37" x 48" piece of batting

Cutting

All measurements include ¼"-wide seam allowances.

From *each* of the charm squares for handles, cut:
9 rectangles, 1" x 2" (you'll need 81 for 27 blocks, 84 for 28 blocks)

From the yellow-dotted fabric, cut:
11 strips, 1½" x 42"; crosscut into:
 54 squares, 1½" x 1½" (56 for 28 blocks)
 27 rectangles, 1½" x 2" (28 for 28 blocks)
 20 rectangles, 1½" x 5" (21 for 28 blocks)
 24 rectangles, 1½" x 6½"
3 strips, 2" x 42"; crosscut into:
 27 rectangles, 1" x 2" (28 for 28 blocks)
 27 squares, 2" x 2" (28 for 28 blocks)
4 strips, 2½" x 42"; crosscut into:
 2 strips, 2½" x 38"
 2 strips, 2½" x 31½"
1 rectangle, 5" x 7½" (you can substitute 1 pieced block and 1 rectangle, 1½" x 5")

From the black-dotted fabric, cut:
1 strip, 1½" x 42"; crosscut into 18 squares, 1½" x 1½"
4 strips, 2¼" x 42"

Making the Blocks

Each block requires one charm square; three matching or coordinating rectangles, 1" x 2", from charm fabric; and two squares, 1½" x 1½", one square, 2" x 2", one rectangle, 1" x 2", and one rectangle, 1½" x 2", from the background fabric.

1 Sew yellow-dotted 1½" squares to two adjacent corners of the charm square, right sides together and stitching diagonally from corner to corner. Trim the excess fabric and press the seam allowances toward the triangles. Repeat with all the charm squares to make 27 cup units.

2 Match the charm squares with coordinating or matching handle rectangles. Sew a handle 1" x 2" rectangle to a yellow-dotted 1" x 2" rectangle. Sew a matching 1" x 2" rectangle to a yellow-dotted 1½" x 2" rectangle. Sew a third matching 1" x 2" rectangle to a yellow-dotted 2" square. Press each unit toward the darker fabric. Sew the three units together as shown. Press. Make 27 handle units.

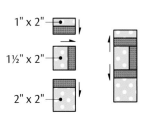

1" x 2"
1½" x 2"
2" x 2"

3 Sew a cup unit from step 1 to a coordinating or matching handle unit from step 2 to make a Coffee Cup block. Press the seam allowances toward the coffee-cup unit. Repeat to make 27 blocks if you want your quilt to look like the one shown, or make 28 blocks if you don't want a plain square.

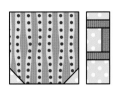 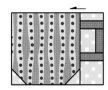

Make 27 or 28.

Assembling the Quilt Top

1 Sew four Coffee Cup blocks in a row, inserting a yellow-dotted 1½" x 5" rectangle between each block. Press the seam allowances toward the yellow-dotted fabric. Make six rows with four cups in each row. For the seventh row, sew the yellow-dotted 5" x 7½" rectangle to the left side of the row instead of a Coffee Cup block and a yellow rectangle.

2 Alternate and sew together four yellow-dotted 1½" x 6" rectangles and three black-dotted squares. Press the seam allowances toward the yellow-dotted fabric. Make six sashing rows.

3 Sew the block and sashing rows together and press the seam allowances toward the sashing rows.

4 Sew the yellow-dotted 2½" x 38" strips to the sides of the quilt and press the seam allowances toward the strips. Sew the 2½" x 31½" strips to the top and bottom of the quilt and press the seam allowances toward the strips.

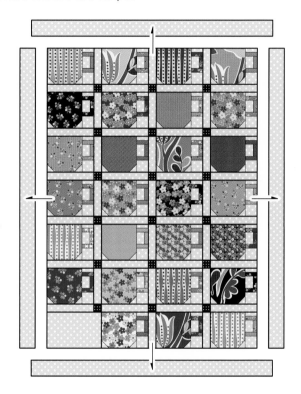

Finishing the Quilt

Go to ShopMartingale.com/HowtoQuilt for more information on finishing your quilt.

1 Layer the quilt top with batting and backing; baste. Quilt as desired.

2 Bind the edges of the quilt using the black-dotted 2¼"-wide strips.

3 Add a hanging sleeve, if desired, and a label.

Table Manners

Everyone will use their best table manners in a dining room graced with this elegant quilt.

Materials

Yardage is based on 42"-wide fabric. Charm squares are 5"x5".

36 charm squares (18 dark and 18 medium)
⅞ yard of aged muslin for background*
¼ yard of dark-blue print for binding
1 yard of fabric for backing
31" x 31" piece of batting

*If aged muslin isn't available, you can substitute regular muslin or an off-white tone-on-tone print.

Cutting

Measurements include ¼"-wide seam allowances. Sort charm squares into pairs of a medium- and a dark-value fabric (two contrasting fabrics).

From *each* charm square, cut:
4 squares, 2⅜" x 2⅜"; cut each square in half diagonally to make 2 triangles (8 per fabric; 288 total). Keep the medium/dark fabric pairs together.

From the muslin, cut:
7 strips, 2⅜" x 42"; cut into 108 squares, 2⅜" x 2⅜". Cut each square in half diagonally to make 2 triangles (216 total).
4 strips, 2" x 42"; cut into 72 squares, 2" x 2"

From the dark-blue print, cut:
3 strips, 2¼" x 42"

Making the Blocks

Work with one medium/dark fabric pair at a time. Each pair will make two identical blocks.

1 Sew a dark fabric triangle and a muslin triangle together as shown. Make three. Repeat with medium fabric triangles and muslin triangles to make three more triangle squares. Make one triangle square with a dark and a medium triangle. Press the seam allowances toward the darker fabrics.

Make 3.   Make 3.   Make 1.

2 Arrange the triangle squares from step 1 with two muslin squares, being careful to position the dark and medium triangles accurately. Sew the units into rows; then sew the rows together. Press. You may find that pressing the seam allowances open makes it easier to match the points. Repeat to make 36 blocks (18 sets of two identical blocks).

Make 2 identical blocks.

By Mary Etherington and Connie Tesene of Country Threads

Quilt size: 27" x 27" • **Block size:** 4½" x 4½"

3 Choose two sets of two identical blocks for each four-block unit. Position the blocks to form a muslin center diamond and sew together. Press. Make nine four-block units.

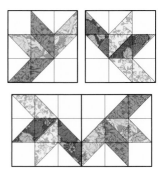

4-block unit.
Make 9.

Assembling the Quilt Top

Sew the four-block units together into three rows of three units each. Press the seam allowances in opposite directions from row to row. Sew the rows together and press.

Finishing the Quilt

Go to ShopMartingale.com/HowtoQuilt for more information on finishing your quilt.

1 Layer the quilt top with batting and backing; baste. Quilt as desired.

2 Bind the edges of the quilt using the dark-blue 2¼"-wide strips.

3 Add a hanging sleeve, if desired, and a label.

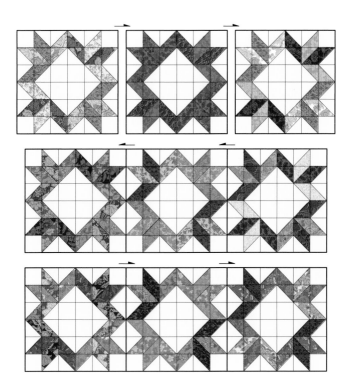

By Mary Etherington and Connie Tesene of Country Threads

Quilt size: 15" x 24" • **Block size:** 3" x 3"

Bursting with Color

This quilt is simply bursting with energy! The flash of turquoise against the hot orange and yellow looks terrific.

Materials

Yardage is based on 42"-wide fabric. Charm squares are 5" x 5".

10 light, 10 dark, and 20 medium charm squares for blocks
⅝ yard of fabric for backing
17" x 26" piece of batting

Cutting

Measurements include ¼"-wide seam allowances.

From *each* of the light charm squares, cut:
1 square, 4¼" x 4¼"; cut each square into quarters diagonally to make 4 triangles (40 total)

From *each* of the dark charm squares, cut:
1 square, 4¼" x 4¼"; cut each square into quarters diagonally to make 4 triangles (40 total)

From *each* of the medium charm squares, cut:
1 square, 3⅞" x 3⅞"; cut each square in half diagonally to make 2 triangles (40 total)

From the fabric for backing, cut:
1 piece, 17" x 26"

Making the Quilt Blocks

1 Sew the dark and light triangles together in pairs, stitching along the short edge, with the dark triangle on the left and the light triangle on the right as shown. Mix the fabrics so the combination in each triangle unit is different. Press the seam allowances toward the dark fabric. Make 40 triangle units.

Make 40.

2 Sew a medium triangle to each unit from step 1, stitching along the long edge. Press the seam allowances toward the medium triangles. Blocks should measure 3½" square. Make 40.

Make 40.

Assembling the Quilt Top

1 Lay out the blocks in eight rows of five blocks each, with the medium triangles in the bottom-right corner.

2 Sew the blocks into rows, pressing in opposite direction from row to row. Sew the rows together and press.

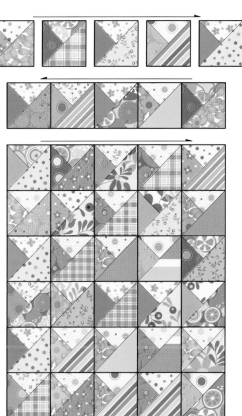

Finishing the Quilt

This quilt doesn't have binding. Instead, the layers are stitched together and turned right side out before quilting.

1 Layer the batting, followed by the backing fabric *right side up,* and then the quilt top *right side down.* The batting and backing are a little larger than the quilt. Pin the layers together around the perimeter of the quilt top.

2 Stitch around the edge of the quilt using a ¼" seam allowance and leaving a 6" opening for turning the quilt right side out.

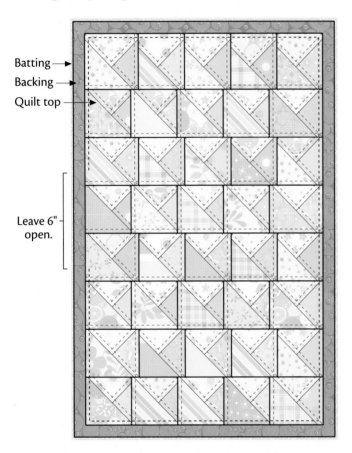

Batting →
Backing →
Quilt top →

Leave 6" open.

3 Trim the batting and backing to the size of the quilt top and clip the excess batting out of the corners to reduce bulk.

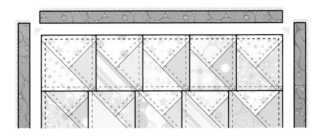

4 Turn the quilt right side out and stitch the opening closed by hand.

5 Press the quilt, and then quilt as desired.

6 Add a hanging sleeve, if desired, and a label.

Dress for Success

There are several ways to make triangle squares, also known as half-square-triangle units. The method employed in this quilt makes the most of the charm squares.

Materials

Yardage is based on 42"-wide fabric. Charm squares are 5" x 5".

38 medium-light to dark charm squares
⅓ yard of light print for block background
⅓ yard of dark-brown print for sashing
⅛ yard of salmon print for cornerstones
⅜ yard of brown print for binding
1 yard of fabric for backing
33" x 33" piece of batting

Cutting

Measurements include ¼"-wide seam allowances.

Select the two lightest charm squares to be used as background squares in two of the blocks. Separate the remaining 36 squares into two stacks: 18 medium and 18 dark.

From *each* of the 18 medium charm squares, cut:
1 square, 4½" x 4½" (18 total)

From the light print, cut:
2 strips, 5" x 42"; crosscut into 16 squares, 5" x 5"

From the dark-brown print, cut:
7 strips, 1½" x 42"; crosscut into 60 strips, 1½" x 4½"

From the salmon print, cut:
1 strip, 1½" x 42"; crosscut into 25 squares, 1½" x 1½"

From the brown print, cut:
3 strips, 2¼" x 42"*

*If you don't have a 42" width of usable fabric, you may need 4 strips.

Making the Blocks

1 Pair each of the 18 dark charm squares right sides together with a light 5" square. (Remember, two of the background squares will be from your charm pack and a little different than your other background squares.)

2 Cut each dark/light pair into quarters that measure 2½" x 2½". Keep squares of the same fabrics together.

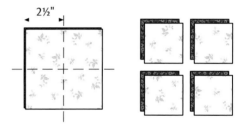

2½"

3 With the light fabric on top, mark a diagonal line from corner to corner on the paired 2½" squares. Stitch along the line. Trim, leaving a ¼" seam allowance. Press the seam allowances toward the dark fabric. Make four matching triangle squares.

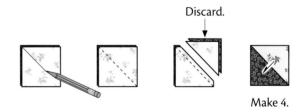

Discard.

Make 4.

4 Combine the four matching triangle squares into a block as shown; press. Repeat to complete 18 blocks.

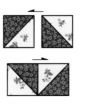

Make 18.

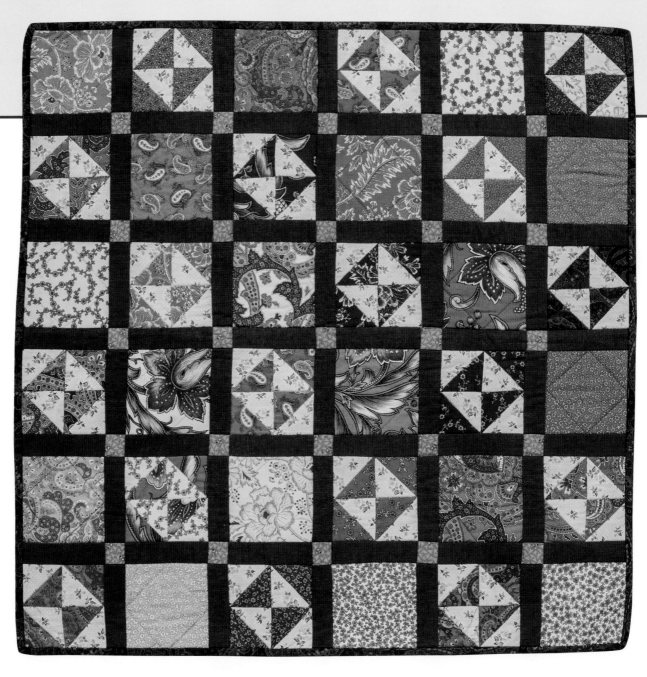

By Mary Etherington and Connie Tesene of Country Threads

Quilt size: 29" x 29" • **Block size:** 4" x 4"

Assembling the Quilt Top

1 Arrange the blocks, alternating with the medium 4½" squares, in six rows of six each. Place a 1½" x 4½" sashing strip between each to make a block row.

2 Alternate six dark-brown 4½"-wide sashing strips with salmon 1½" cornerstones as shown to make a sashing row.

3 Sew into rows, and then sew the rows together. Press as shown.

Finishing the Quilt

Go to ShopMartingale.com/HowtoQuilt for more information on finishing your quilt.

1 Layer the quilt top with batting and backing; baste. Quilt as desired.

2 Bind the edges of the quilt using the brown 2¼"-wide strips.

3 Add a hanging sleeve, if desired, and a label.

By Mary Etherington and Connie Tesene of Country Threads

Quilt size: 24" x 24" • **Block size:** 4" x 4"

Easy Holiday Treat

A perfect gift for the hectic holidays, this quilt won't take too much time and is simple to make. You might even get it made without being interrupted!

Materials

Yardage is based on 42"-wide fabric. Charm squares are 5" x 5".

33 Christmas print charm squares for blocks
¼ yard of brown Christmas print for border
¼ yard of dark-red print for binding and blocks
1 yard of fabric for backing
28" x 28" piece of batting

Cutting

Measurements include ¼"-wide seam allowances.

From *each* of the charm squares, cut:

3 rectangles, 1½" x 4½" (99 total; see cutting illustration)

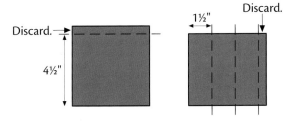

From the brown Christmas print, cut:
2 strips, 2½" x 20½"
2 strips, 2½" x 24½"

From the dark-red print, cut:
3 strips, 2¼" x 42"
1 rectangle, 1½" x 4½"

Careful Color Placement

Take care to position the red (or your most dominant color) strips on the outside edge of most of your blocks so that when they're set together, you can form the rail fence pattern that runs through the quilt top.

Making the Blocks

Sew the 1½" x 4½" rectangles together in pairs. (One rectangle comes from the dark-red binding fabric.) Sew two pairs together to make a four-rectangle block. Repeat to make 25 blocks total.

Make 25.

Assembling the Quilt Top

1 Lay out the blocks in five rows of five blocks each, alternating the direction of the rails from horizontal to vertical. Study the diagrams when placing the red strips. If you choose to discard a red strip that isn't as dark as the others, you can use leftover dark-red binding fabric for the red rails.

2 When you're satisfied with the block arrange-ment, sew the blocks into rows. Press the seam allowances toward the vertical blocks. Sew the rows together. Press.

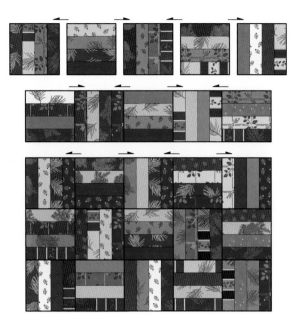

3 Sew the brown 20½"-long strips to the top and bottom of the quilt top and press the seam allow-ances toward the borders. Repeat using the brown 24½"-long strips for the sides of the quilt.

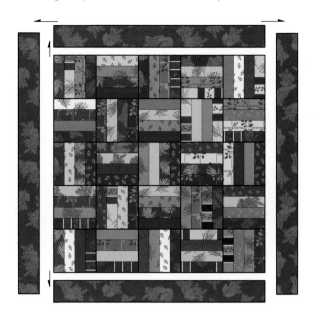

Finishing the Quilt

Go to ShopMartingale.com/HowtoQuilt for more information on finishing your quilt.

1 Layer the quilt top with batting and backing; baste. Quilt as desired.

2 Bind the edges of the quilt using the dark-red 2¼"-wide strips.

3 Add a hanging sleeve, if desired, and a label.

Charming Squares and Diamonds

This intricate-looking quilt couldn't be easier. Diamonds are free-form cut, fused in place over a quilt top of pieced squares, and secured with a decorative machine stitch.

Materials

Yardage is based on 42"-wide fabric. Charm squares are 5"x5".

48 assorted light charm squares for background

⅝ yards of pink tone-on-tone print for diamond appliqués and binding

1 yard of fabric for backing

33" x 42" piece of batting

1⅓ yards of 12"-wide lightweight paper-backed fusible web (such as Steam-A-Seam 2)

Cutting

Measurements include a ¼"-wide seam allowance.

From the pink tone-on-tone print, cut:
4 strips, 2¼" x 42"

Apply fusible web to the wrong side of the remaining pink tone-on-tone print, and cut:
6 strips, 1½" wide; crosscut into 58 rectangles, 1½" x 4½"

Assembling the Quilt Top

1 Randomly arrange the 5" squares into eight rows of six squares each. Sew the squares in each row together. Press the seam allowances in opposite directions from row to row. Sew the rows together. Press the seam allowances in one direction.

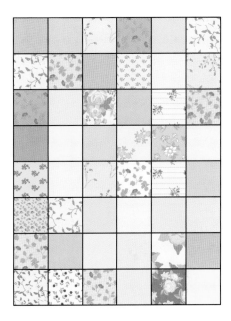

2 Layer the quilt top with batting and backing. Baste the layers together. Using a thread that blends with all of the fabrics, stitch in the ditch of all of the seams.

3 Fold a pink 1½" x 4½" rectangle in half along the long edges to make a piece 1½" x 2¼". Then fold the piece in half at the short raw edges and finger crease the fold to mark the center. Using a rotary cutter or scissors, cut from the outside edge of the fold to the center mark on each side of the rectangle. Repeat with the remaining rectangles to make a total of 58 diamonds. Remove the paper backing from each diamond.

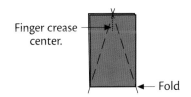

Finger crease center.

Fold

By Terry Martin

Quilt size: 27" x 36" • **Block size:** 4½" x 4½"

4 Place a diamond directly over every inside seam except those on the outer squares, with the points meeting at the intersections as shown. Refer to the manufacturer's instructions to fuse the diamonds in place.

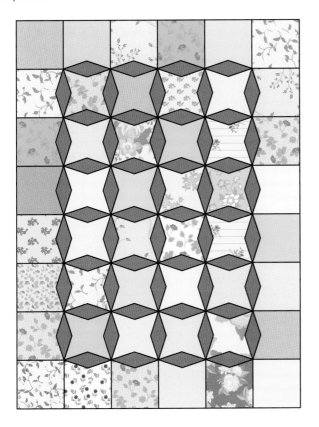

5 Using a decorative machine stitch, stitch over the raw edges of the diamonds. For best results sew down the side of one row, and then with the needle down, pivot 180° and sew back up the other side of the diamonds in that row. Start with the center row and work outward.

Finishing the Quilt

Go to ShopMartingale.com/HowtoQuilt for more information on finishing your quilt.

1 Add additional machine quilting as desired.

2 Bind the edges of the quilt using the pink 2¼"-wide strips.

3 Add a hanging sleeve, if desired, and a label.

Designed and pieced by Barbara Groves and Mary Jacobson
Quilt size: 50" x 50" • **Block size:** 8" x 8"

Aunt Bea

Get the chicken frying . . . Barney's coming to dinner! This easy, nostalgic quilt is made using feedsack and 1950s-style prints. One simple block is all you'll need to create this fun down-home quilt.

Materials

Yardage is based on 42"-wide fabric. Charm squares are 5" x 5".

50 coordinating charm squares for blocks
1⅞ yards of red print for blocks and border
½ yard of plaid fabric for binding
3¼ yards of fabric for backing
58" x 58" piece of batting
25 white buttons for embellishment
1 skein of red embroidery floss for tying buttons

Cutting

Measurements include a ¼"-wide seam allowance.

From the red print, cut:
13 strips, 2½" x 42"; crosscut into 50 rectangles,
   2½" x 8½"
5 strips, 5¼" x 42"

From the plaid fabric, cut:
6 strips, 2¼" x 42"

Making the Blocks

1 Divide the 50 charm squares into 25 pairs of contrasting colors or contrasting values (light and dark). Layer each pair of squares right sides together and, using a ¼" seam allowance, stitch along two opposite sides of the squares as shown.

2 Cut through the center of the squares, parallel to the seams, and press the seam allowances open. Make a total of 50 two-patch units.

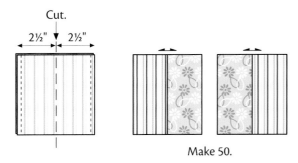

Make 50.

3 Divide the 50 two-patch units from step 2 into 25 new combinations of contrasting pairs. With right sides together, layer the two-patch units, aligning the seams. Using a ¼" seam allowance, stitch along two opposite sides, making sure to stitch across the previous seam lines as shown.

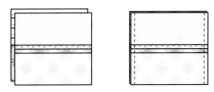

4 Cut through the center of the sewn units and press the seam allowances open. Make a total of 50 Four Patch blocks.

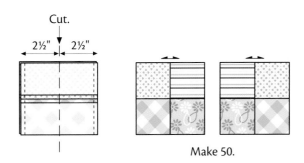

Make 50.

5 Arrange and sew two Four Patch blocks and two red-print 2½" x 8½" rectangles into units as shown. The units should measure 8½" x 8½" square. Make a total of 25.

Make 25.

Assembling the Quilt Top

1 Arrange the units into five rows of five units each, alternating the direction of the units as shown.

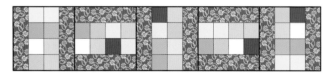

Make 3.

Make 2.

2 Sew the rows together referring to the quilt assembly diagram above right. The quilt should now measure 40½" x 40½".

3 Piece the five red-print 5¼" x 40" border strips together end to end.

4 Measure the quilt from top to bottom through the middle to determine the length of the side borders. From the pieced strip, cut side borders to the needed length and attach them to the sides of the quilt.

5 Measure the quilt from side to side through the middle, including the side borders, to determine the length of the top and bottom borders. From the pieced strip, cut the top and bottom borders to the needed length and attach them to the top and bottom of the quilt.

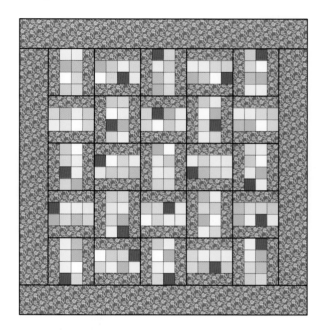

Finishing the Quilt

Go to ShopMartingale.com/HowtoQuilt for more information on finishing your quilt.

1 Layer the quilt top with batting and backing; baste. Quilt as desired.

2 Bind the edges of the quilt using the plaid 2¼"-wide strips.

3 Decorate the quilt with your favorite buttons and tie them on using a needle and embroidery floss.

4 Add a hanging sleeve, if desired, and a label.

Gum Chain

Did you know that the world's longest gum-wrapper chain is 52,913 feet long and contains 1,240,000 gum wrappers? This quilt is reminiscent of a colorful paper chain.

Materials

Yardage is based on 42"-wide fabric. Charm squares are 5"x5".

78 coordinating charm squares for blocks
⅝ yard *each* of yellow, orange, pink, purple, turquoise, and green prints for blocks
1¼ yards of turquoise print for border
⅝ yard of turquoise print for binding
5¼ yards of fabric for backing
69" x 89" piece of batting

Cutting

Measurements include ¼"-wide seam allowances.

From the yellow print, cut:
4 strips, 4½" x 42"; crosscut into:
   12 rectangles, 4½" x 8½"
   2 squares, 4½" x 4½"

From the orange print, cut:
4 strips, 4½" x 42"; crosscut into:
   12 rectangles, 4½" x 8½"
   2 squares, 4½" x 4½"

From the pink print, cut:
4 strips, 4½" x 42"; crosscut into:
   12 rectangles, 4½" x 8½"
   2 squares, 4½" x 4½"

From the purple print, cut:
4 strips, 4½" x 42"; crosscut into:
   12 rectangles, 4½" x 8½"
   2 squares, 4½" x 4½"

From the turquoise print for blocks, cut:
4 strips, 4½" x 42"; crosscut into 13 rectangles,
   4½" x 8½"

From the green print, cut:
4 strips, 4½" x 42"; crosscut into 13 rectangles,
   4½" x 8½"

From the turquoise print for border, cut:
8 strips, 4¾" x 42"

From the turquoise print for binding, cut:
8 strips, 2¼" x 42"

Making the Blocks

1 Divide the 78 coordinating charm squares into 39 pairs of contrasting colors or values (light and dark). Layer each pair of squares right sides together and, using a ¼" seam allowance, stitch along two opposite sides of the squares as shown.

2 Cut through the center of the squares, parallel to the seams, and press the seam allowances open. Make a total of 78 two-patch units.

Cut.

2½"   2½"

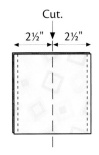 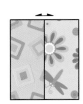 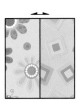

Make 78.

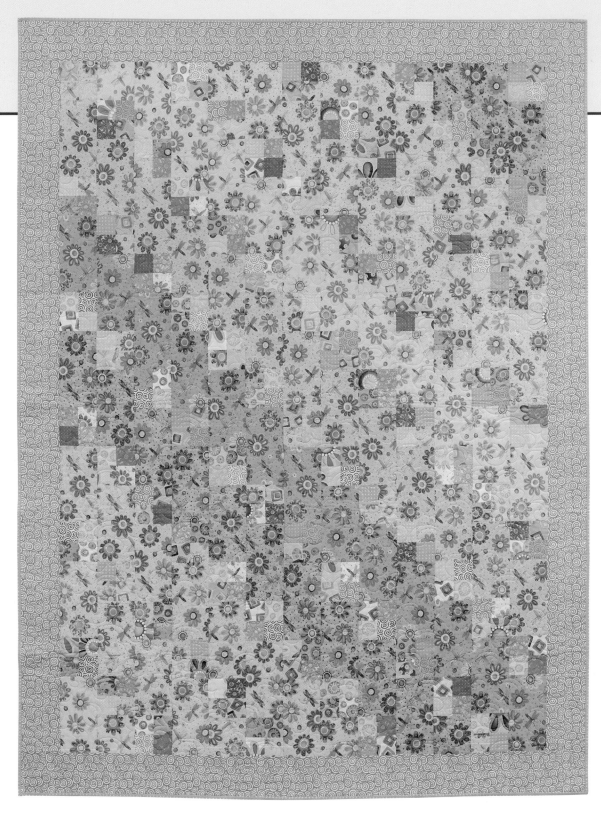

Designed and pieced by Mary Jacobson and Barbara Groves
Quilt size: 61" x 81" • Block size: 4" x 4"

3 Divide the 78 two-patch units from step 2 into 39 new combinations of contrasting pairs. With right sides together, layer the two-patch units, aligning the seams. Using a ¼" seam allowance, stitch along two opposite sides, making sure to stitch across the previous seam lines as shown.

4 Cut through the center of the sewn units as shown and press the seam allowances open. Make a total of 78 Four Patch blocks. The blocks should measure 4½" x 4½".

Cut.

2½" 2½"

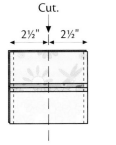

Make 78.

Assembling the Quilt Top

1 Referring to the diagram below, arrange and sew the Four Patch blocks, the rectangles, and the squares into 13 vertical rows as shown. Sew the rows together. The quilt center should now measure 52½" x 72½".

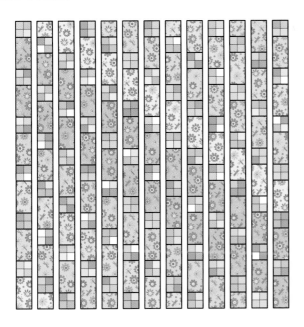

2 Piece the eight turquoise 4¾" x 42" border strips together end to end.

3 Measure the quilt from top to bottom through the middle to determine the length of the side borders. From the pieced strip, cut two side borders to the needed length and attach them to the sides of the quilt.

4 Measure the quilt from side to side through the middle including the side borders to determine the length of the top and bottom borders. From the pieced strip, cut the top and bottom borders to the needed length and attach them to the top and bottom of the quilt.

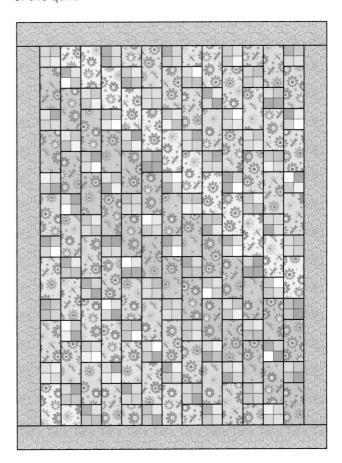

Finishing the Quilt

Go to ShopMartingale.com/HowtoQuilt for more information on finishing your quilt.

1 Layer the quilt top with batting and backing, baste. Quilt as desired.

2 Bind the edges of the quilt using the turquoise 2¼"-wide strips.

3 Add a hanging sleeve, if desired, and a label.

By Mary Etherington and Connie Tesene of Country Threads

Quilt size: 30" x 30" • **Block size:** 9" x 9"

Folded-Corner Charms

Sewing a small polka-dot square to the corner of each charm square before joining the charms together gives this easy quilt an added sense of whimsy.

Materials

Yardage is based on 42"-wide fabric. Charm squares are 5" x 5".

36 assorted charm squares in your favorite prints
⅜ yard of brown polka-dot print for block connector squares and border
⅓ yard of dark-brown print for binding
1⅛ yards of fabric for backing
36" x 36" piece of batting

Cutting

Measurements include ¼"-wide seam allowances.

From the brown polka-dot, cut:
2 strips, 2½" x 42"; crosscut into 36 squares, 2½" x 2½"
4 strips, 2" x 42"

From the dark-brown print, cut:
4 strips, 2¼" x 42"

Making the Blocks

1 Sew a brown polka-dot 2½" square to one corner of each of the charm squares as shown. Trim the outside corner, leaving a ¼" seam allowance. Press the seam allowances toward the triangles.

Make 36.

2 Sew four of the units from step 1 together to make a block, arranging the dark triangles to meet in the center. Press the seam allowances in opposite directions. Repeat to make nine blocks.

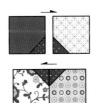

Make 9.

Assembling the Quilt Top

1 Sew the blocks together into three rows of three blocks per row. Press the seam allowances in opposite directions from row to row. Sew the rows together and press.

2 Measure the length of the quilt, cut two of the brown polka-dot 2" x 42" strips to this width, and sew them to the sides of the quilt. Press the seam allowances toward the strips. Measure the width of the quilt. Cut the remaining 2"-wide strips to this length and sew them to the top and bottom of the quilt. Press the seam allowances toward the strips.

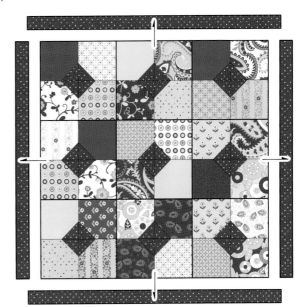

Finishing the Quilt

Go to ShopMartingale.com/HowtoQuilt for more information on finishing your quilt.

1 Layer the quilt top with batting and backing; baste. Quilt as desired.

2 Bind the edges of the quilt using the dark-brown 2¼"-wide strips.

3 Add a hanging sleeve, if desired, and a label.

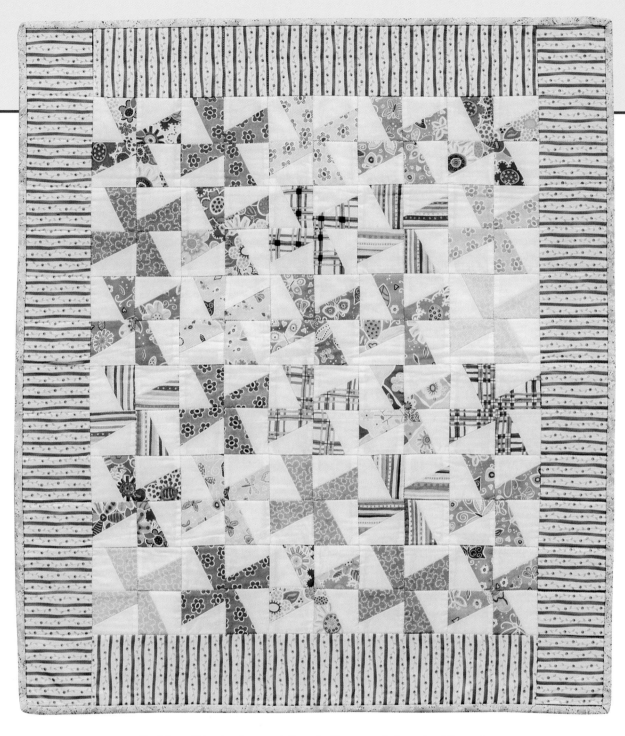

By Mary Etherington and Connie Tesene of Country Threads

Quilt size: 26" x 30" • **Block size:** 4" x 4"

Windmill Charm

Use a charm pack of children's prints or other bright and cheerful fabric for this delightful little quilt.

Materials

Yardage is based on 42"-wide fabric. Charm squares are 5"x5".

30 medium- to light-pastel charm squares for blocks
½ yard of white fabric for block background
½ yard of blue-and-white striped fabric for border
¼ yard of pink print for binding
1 yard of fabric for backing
30" x 34" piece of batting
2½" square of template plastic*

A mini windmill acrylic template for 4" scraps is also available. Check your local quilt shop or at www.CountryThreads.com.

Cutting

Measurements include ¼"-wide seam allowances.

From *each* charm square, cut:
2 rectangles, 2½" x 5" (60 total)

From the white fabric, cut:
5 strips, 2½" x 42"

From the blue-and-white striped fabric, cut:
2 strips, 3½" x 30½"
2 strips, 3½" x 20½"

From the pink print, cut:
3 strips, 2¼" x 42"

Making the Blocks

1 Make a plastic template of the windmill blade pattern on page 32.

2 Layer two to four pastel 2½" x 5" rectangles, all right side up, being careful to align all the edges. Use the template to mark two windmill blades on the top fabric. Then use your rotary cutter and ruler to cut on the marked lines through all the layers. Cut all the pastel rectangles in the same manner; you'll have four windmill blades from each fabric (120 total).

3 If your white fabric has a discernable right and wrong side, cut the 2½"-wide strips in half along the fold line and lay them on top of each other, all with right side facing up and the edges carefully aligned. (If both sides are identical you can leave the fabric strips folded.) Trace the windmill blade template across the top strip as shown and cut 120 white windmill blades.

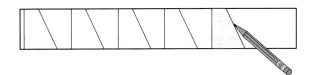

4 Join each pastel windmill blade with a white windmill blade. The pieces align at the ¼" seam and along the diagonal side. Press the seam allowances toward the charm fabric. Make 120 windmill-blade units (30 sets of four with the same fabric).

Make 30 sets
of 4 each (120 total).

5 Join four units with the same fabric as shown. Press the long seam allowances open to reduce bulk. Repeat to make 30 blocks.

Make 30.

Assembling the Quilt Top

1 Lay out the blocks in six rows of five blocks each. Sew the blocks into rows, and then sew the rows together. Press in the opposite direction from row to row.

2 Sew the striped 3½" x 20½" strips to the quilt top and bottom. Press the seam allowances toward the borders. Sew the striped 3½" x 30½" strips to the sides of the quilt. Press the seam allowances toward the borders.

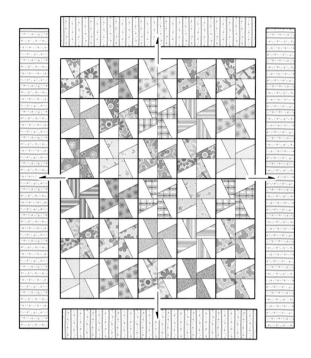

Finishing the Quilt

Go to ShopMartingale.com/HowtoQuilt for more information on finishing your quilt.

1 Layer the quilt top with batting and backing; baste. Quilt as desired.

2 Bind the edges of the quilt using the pink 2¼"-wide strips.

3 Add a hanging sleeve, if desired, and a label.

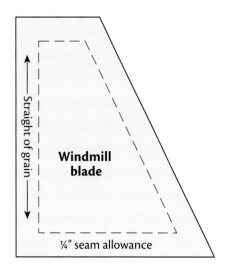

Straight of grain

Windmill blade

¼" seam allowance